All proceeds benefit Woodlands Wildlife Refuge

To Jake, Charlie & Conner,
Enjoy!
Loren Spiotta-DiMare

K. Wilde

Dedication

This book is dedicated to the hundreds of thousands of wild animals affected by human encounters that arrive at wildlife rehabilitation facilities around the world each year, to those who discover them and care enough to pause and find help, and to those tireless, compassionate and often under-appreciated wildlife rehabilitators and volunteers saving one wild life at a time. Each animal found and cared for touches the lives of many and offers the opportunity to educate people about our wild neighbors in a unique way. *Broke Leg Bear* is a perfect example of what a difference just one animal can make.

I am deeply grateful for the opportunity to have helped so many incredible wild creatures. I thank them deeply for what they have taught me and wish their wild spirits well, whether walking this earth or not.

This story would not be possible without the generosity and support that has made Woodlands Wildlife Refuge the success it is today. As Woodlands celebrates 25 years, I thank beyond words each and every person that has shown and given each and every kindness! Please know that you have made an incredible difference.

Tracy Leaver, Founder and Executive Director
Woodlands Wildlife Refuge

This book was made possible through the generosity of:
Alice Lauyer
Karianne and Eric Marshall
Sandy and Karolee Glassman

and the creative expertise and generosity of:
Author Loren Spiotta-DiMare
Illustrator Key Wilde
Designer Vanessa Gieske

Broke Leg Bear

A True Story

By Loren Spiotta-DiMare

Illustrated By Key Wilde

The large, black bear ambles along a path in the woods. Hungry and thirsty, she's headed for the river. Her cub trails close behind. When they reach the highway, the mother bear watches for cars. She understands the dangers of the road. Now it's safe. She darts across in just a few strides. But her cub is no longer by her side.

Catching the scent of juicy, ripe berries hanging from some nearby shrubs, the young bear has paused to snack.

Suddenly the cub realizes she's lost sight of her mother. She dashes across the road to find her. Seconds later she hears a honking horn and screeching brakes. The driver swerves trying not to hit the baby bear, but the front of the car bumps into her back leg. The woman quickly dials 911 as the bear lies on the side of the road, breathing but very still.

A police officer arrives on the scene in minutes. "I tried not to hit her," the woman cries out. "But she came out of nowhere–running so fast."

"You did the right thing–by calling 911," the officer says. "I got in touch with the Bear Team at New Jersey Fish and Wildlife. One of their biologists is on his way." Just then a truck pulls up. A Fish and Wildlife biologist jumps out and hurries over to the cub. "She's in bad shape," he says to the officer and the driver. "I'll take her to Woodlands Wildlife Refuge. They can help her."

Did You Know?

Woodlands Wildlife Refuge is a rehabilitation center and hospital for wild animals. Tracy Leaver is a state-licensed wildlife rehabilitator. While wildlife rehabilitation centers can be found in most states, Woodlands is the only one allowed to work with black bears in New Jersey.

The cub stirs as the two men gently load her onto a stretcher and into the truck. Softly, the officer says, "It looks like one of her back legs is broken." The biologist agrees and replies, "I'll call Tracy at Woodlands as soon as I get on the road. She'll know what to do." The driver thanks the men for arriving so quickly.

When the biologist reaches Woodlands, Tracy is waiting. Together they place the cub in a cage. Tracy examines her quickly and confirms the leg is broken. She gives the cub some medicine to help with her pain.

"Thank you for bringing her to us. We'll do all we can for her," Tracy says to the biologist as he heads back to his truck.

Knowing the cub's injury is serious she calls Dr. Eric Glass at Red Bank Veterinary Hospital, one of the largest pet animal hospitals in the country. Dr. Glass is a neurologist who helped another bear cub and a coyote from Woodlands. Tracy arranges to have the injured bear driven to the hospital the following day.

"This can be fixed," Dr. Glass says to himself as he examines the cub. He brings in Dr. Garrett Davis, an orthopedic surgeon. "It's not often I treat wild animals," Dr. Davis says. "But I try to help those who do arrive at the hospital."

"The cub had a bad break in her thigh bone. I was able to fix it surgically by attaching a steel plate and twelve screws to keep the leg in proper position."

The young bear stays in the hospital for three days. She sits quietly in her cage and seems a little scared and shy. She looks warily at anyone who walks through the surgery ward but never appears to feel threatened.

Both Dr. Glass and Dr. Davis are very happy to have saved the young bear's life. "It was a great experience to help her," Dr. Davis says.

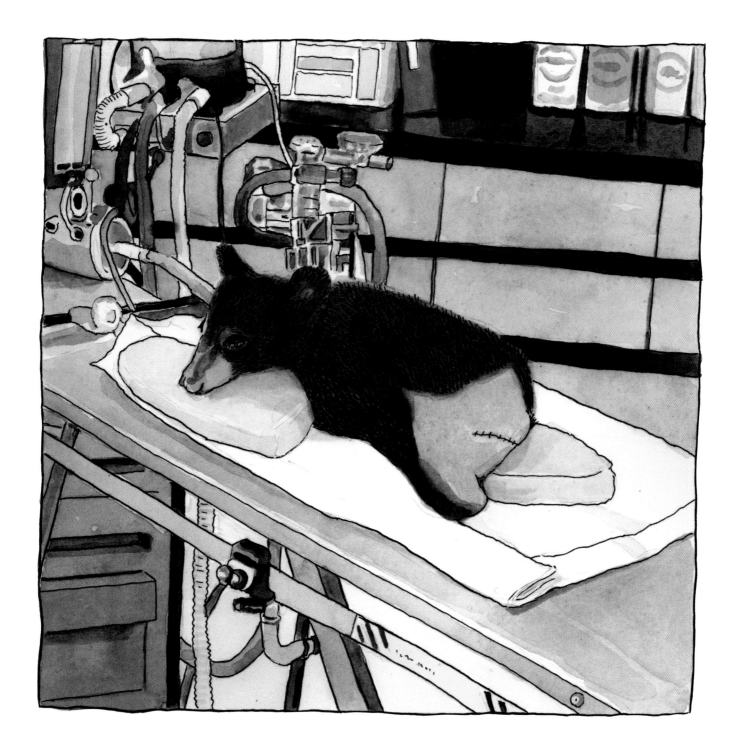

When the cub returns to Woodlands, the staff and volunteers name her "Broke Leg." They place her in a small cage so she won't move around too much and re-injure herself. She's watched carefully and given her medicine hidden in grapes. She snuggles and sleeps with her paw around a soft toy animal.

Each day Broke Leg becomes stronger and starts to notice all the young animals in the hospital nursery with her. It's baby season at Woodlands. Broke Leg is amazed to see chipmunks, rabbits, raccoons, squirrels and many other orphans. Some are so young, they are fed by volunteers with special syringes or baby bottles. Broke Leg likes the company of these other animals.

Did You Know?

Most of the animals arrive at Woodlands due to human causes such as construction, cars, pets, lawnmowers and tree cutting.

One morning, Broke Leg notices Roomba, an African tortoise munching on dandelions. Tracy explains to a visitor how Roomba was found on a golf course. "We believe he must have been someone's pet at one time," she says. "Because *African* tortoises certainly don't live in New Jersey!"

Roomba will spend the rest of his life in captivity at Woodlands. He takes part in the education program. It's his "job" to remind people that wild animals should never be turned into pets. Roomba is happy to be at Woodlands, slowly roaming the grounds and receiving lots of attention from everyone there.

On a hot summer day, soon after Broke Leg discovered Roomba, she hears loud noises outside the nursery. Eight more bear cubs have arrived at Woodlands! One is sitting in Tracy's lap as she presses wet towels on his head and stomach to keep him cool. The cub is crying, calling for his mother. So are the others. They're sad and confused.

There have never been so many cubs at the refuge at one time! Tracy explains to her staff and volunteers that the cubs' mothers were destroyed because they turned into *nuisance bears*, frightening people by coming into their yards or breaking into homes looking for food.

"It was hot. They were scared, and we were heartbroken about why they had come to us. Several days went by before they stopped crying and became less afraid," Tracy recalls. "And we only had room for five bears so a much larger enclosure had to be built."

It would take time and a lot of money to build! Luckily, local newspaper reporters had taken an interest in so many bears arriving at Woodlands. Once the news about the orphaned cubs appeared in newspapers, people from all over the area began to send in donations to help them.

Did You Know?

Wild animals fed by people near populated areas can create dangerous situations for themselves, household pets, and humans.

Broke Leg is having some problems of her own. Three weeks after her surgery, she is still not using her injured leg. The staff and volunteers are worried because the cub's recovery is taking longer than expected. Then, little by little, Broke Leg works her leg into a normal position until one afternoon. . .she stands! Everyone is very excited. It's a triumphant day for Broke Leg.

Now she's able to move to a larger cage outside, which gives her more room to stretch and strengthen her leg. There's a plastic igloo in the cage which makes a nice den.

One morning Broke Leg hears a very loud meow. It's Lady Jane, the Canadian lynx. The large cat is excited to see her favorite volunteers, Ellen and Jackie, who are walking toward her. She's so happy to see them, she starts to pace and cry out.

Then Broke Leg notices a very small, adult bear. Her name is Grace. Like Roomba, Lady Jane and Grace cannot be returned to the wild. So they too have become part of the education program at Woodlands.

Did You Know?

Some animals that come to Woodlands can never be released, so they become part of the education program and help teach people about wild animals.

A month after Broke Leg moves outside, another lone cub arrives at Woodlands. He was found wandering along a road without his mother. This cub is quite feisty and quickly earns the name, "Wicked." The staff decides to put him together with Broke Leg. Having another cub to play with will help strengthen her leg even more.

Everyone is curious to see how the two will get along. At first, Broke Leg *bluff charges*—stomping her feet and snapping her jaws. This is how bears warn other animals to stay away. Then she hides inside her igloo and does her best to ignore Wicked.

Wicked climbs on top of the igloo and gently, reaches down with his paw, trying to touch Broke Leg again and again. Just as often, she smacks away his paw and snorts. But by the end of the day the two cubs become friends.

The better Broke Leg begins to feel, the more bear-like she becomes—defending her home by bluff charging. Her caretakers have to be very clever in how they feed her and the other bears. So volunteers stuff their meals—mainly dog food, fruit, vegetables, and acorns—into pumpkins or hide the food under brush, logs and rocks. That way, everything scatters and encourages foraging. "Our goal is to return the animals to the wild able to take care of themselves," Tracy explains to a new volunteer. "So we must be careful not to treat them as pets."

Did You Know?

Not being true predators, black bears eat mainly plant matter including grasses, skunk cabbage, nuts and berries. They also enjoy insects like ants and termites and only eat small amounts of meat when they find it easily.

By fall, all of the bear cubs weigh about seventy-five pounds and eat fifteen pounds of food a day. Soon they will outgrow their temporary cages! Plus, the harsh winter weather isn't far off. The Woodlands' staff and volunteers know they have to build an extra large enclosure for all ten bears and there isn't much time.

The project begins in December. Luckily enough donations and supplies have been received. But the hard work is still ahead. Over the next several weeks the staff and friends of Woodlands spend all their free time building a new home for the bears. They work through the holidays, freezing wind, ice and mud. "We'll make it," one volunteer says to another on an especially cold windy day. "We have to," his friend replies.

Finally, in January the bears' new, roomy enclosure is ready! All of the cubs are safely sedated and examined by a Fish and Wildlife biologist from the New Jersey Black Bear Research Team. They are then moved to their new home. By the end of the day as the cubs wake up they begin to explore their new surroundings. They climb the big trees, splash in the stream, wade in the pond and hide in their dens.

Broke Leg and Wicked quickly become friends with the other cubs. Broke Leg is now able to climb, run and play as well as the others. The staff and volunteers watch the cubs acting like true, wild bears. "It was one of the most special days we've ever had at Woodlands," Tracy says. "Truly what our work here is all about."

Did You Know?

Black bears are not true hibernators like woodchucks, but they will sleep through the harsh days of winter, only venturing out on the warmest of days for a quick drink or to forage for a small amount of food.

Over the winter the cubs are sleepy and spend most of their time in their dens. They only come out now and then to find food or take a drink from the stream.

But when spring arrives, the cubs, who are now all yearlings, need more room. They become more active and restless. Pacing along the sides of their enclosure they also play hard and rough with each other. Their caretakers spend less time with them as they will soon be old enough to move back to their wild world. All the cubs will be released near where they were found, but not too close to people.

On their big day, Broke Leg and the other yearling bears are sedated for the last time and given a final health exam. Each is weighed and has a special number tattooed inside its lip and stamped on its ear tag. Females are given radio collars, that will eventually fall off, so they can be followed after their release. Radio collars are not given to males since they like to travel very far. The bears are then placed in metal cylinders and loaded into a truck for their trip to a carefully chosen release site that has plenty of natural food and water.

"Ladies and gentleman, the largest release of black bears in the state of New Jersey," announces black bear biologist Kelcey Burguess. The bears, awake now, can be heard banging around inside their cylinders, restless and ready to get out

The trapdoors open. The bears leap from the cylinders and in an instant disappear into the nearby woods. They are finally home, wild and free as they were meant to be. One, perhaps Broke Leg, stops briefly, forepaws on a tree and looks back at all the people who helped the orphaned cubs, as if to say, "Good-bye and thank you."

Epilogue

As part of their bear research, the Woodlands' staff and the New Jersey Black Bear Team keep track of all the bears after they are released to make sure they are living well. Once their radio collars fall off, the tags and tattoos identify the bears. Some have been tracked for up to ten years and have had litters that are now being tracked. Since 1995 Woodlands has rehabilitated and released over sixty black bears and not one has become a nuisance or problem bear.

Months after returning to the woods and shortly before her radio collar dropped off, Broke Leg was spotted foraging near her release site. Perhaps, one day, she will have cubs of her own.

Glossary

amble	a leisurely, walking pace
biologist	one who studies the lives of animals and plants
captivity	to be held in a man-made environment—not able to live in the wild
cylinder	long, rounded box
enclosure	to shut in all around for example a pen or cage
feisty	lively, full of spirit
foraging	to search for food
orphaned	without parents
neurologist	a doctor who deals with the brain and nervous system
nuisance	cause trouble
orthopedic surgeon	a doctor who corrects problems with bones and joints with surgery
sedated	to cause to sleep using medication
syringes	narrow tube, with rubber plunger at one end
temporary	a short time
triumphant	victorious, great success
warily	unsure of
yearling	one-year-old animal

Woodlands Wildlife Refuge®

Since 1986, Woodlands Wildlife Refuge, Inc. located in Hunterdon County, NJ has been dedicated to the care and release of orphaned and injured wild animals. As our communities continue to grow, loss of habitat increases as do human/wild animal encounters resulting in hundreds of wild patients arriving for care each year. These animals include, but are not limited to raccoons, turtles, skunks, foxes, squirrels, woodchucks, mink, otter, bobcats, rabbits, opossums, bats, coyotes, porcupines, and bears. Woodlands is proud to give a second chance to all native mammals and reptiles and remains committed to meeting the needs of wildlife and the communities it serves.

Through its science-based public education programs, Woodlands provides valuable information about wild animals and their habits and habitats.

Woodlands is a 501c3 charity that receives no state or federal money and relies completely on the generosity of others.

For more information about Woodlands Wildlife Refuge, or to make a donation, please visit www.woodlandswildlife.org and become a friend on Facebook.

about the author
Loren Spiotta-DiMare

A life-long animal lover, Loren Spiotta-DiMare has been writing about her favorite subject for over 30 years. She's had five adult books published, *Macaws*, *Siamese Cats*, *The Sporting Spaniel Handbook*, *Beyond The Finish Line: Stories of Ex-Racehorses* and *Cavalier King Charles Spaniel* as well as eight picture books for children including: *Madeline's Miracle*, *Rockwell: A Boy And His Dog*, *Chelsea & The New Puppy*, *Daniel, Dog Camp Champ!*, *Norman To The Rescue*, *Caesar: On Deaf Ears* and *Hannah's House Rabbit*. She is also the co-author of *Everyone Loves Elwood*.

Recognized by the Dog Writers Association of America, Humane Society of the United States, Doris Day Animal Foundation and New Jersey Press Women, Loren's work has been published both nationally and internationally.

In each of her books, the author tries to promote a respect and appreciation for all animals. A resident of Hunterdon County, New Jersey, Loren and her husband, Lou share their home with several beloved dogs and pet birds. Loren's equine companion lives nearby.

photo by Sylvia Bors

about the illustrator
Key Wilde

Key Wilde is a visual artist who also writes and performs original "family" music. The board book/audio CD "Rise and Shine" by Key Wilde & Mr. Clarke (Little Monster Records) received a Parent's Choice Gold Award in 2010. Wilde designed and illustrated the long-running exhibition "Wildlife Wonders! The Animals of Central Park" for the Central Park Conservancy. He lives with his wife and two children in Hunterdon County, New Jersey. View Key's work at www.keywilde.com.